W9-AHJ-301

Backyard Bird Watchers

A Bird Watcher's Guide to

CHICKADEES

By
Mark Harasymiw

Gareth Stevens
PUBLISHING

Please visit our website, www.garethstevens.com. For a free color catalog of all our high-quality books, call toll free 1-800-542-2595 or fax 1-877-542-2596.

Library of Congress Cataloging-in-Publication Data

Harasymiw, Mark, author.
 A bird watcher's guide to chickadees / Mark Harasymiw.
    pages cm. — (Backyard bird watchers)
 Includes bibliographical references and index.
ISBN 978-1-4824-3879-6 (pbk.)
ISBN 978-1-4824-3880-2 (6 pack)
ISBN 978-1-4824-3901-4 (library binding)
1. Chickadees—Juvenile literature. 2. Bird watching—Juvenile literature. I. Title.
 QL696.P2615H36 2016
 598.8'24—dc23
                                        2015018177

First Edition

Published in 2016 by
Gareth Stevens Publishing
111 East 14th Street, Suite 349
New York, NY 10003

Copyright © 2016 Gareth Stevens Publishing

Designer: Laura Bowen
Editor: Therese Shea

Photo credits: Cover, p. 1 (chickadee) Steve Byland/Shutterstock.com; cover, pp. 1–32 (paper texture) javarman/Shutterstock.com; cover, pp. 1–32 (footprints) pio3/Shutterstock.com; pp. 4–29 (note paper) totallyPic.com/Shutterstock.com; pp. 4–29 (photo frame, tape) mtkang/Shutterstock.com; p. 5 Stockbyte/Getty Images; p. 7 Al Mueller/Shutterstock.com; p. 9 KellyNelson/Shutterstock.com; p. 11 Brian Lasenby/Shutterstock.com; p. 12 John E Heintz Jr/Shutterstock.com; p. 13 John Cancalosi/Getty Images; p. 15 Anatoliy Lukich/Shutterstock.com; p. 17 Mgrfan/Wikimedia Commons; p. 19 PookieFugglestein/Wikimedia Commons; p. 21 rck_953/Shutterstock.com; p. 23 Volodymyr Burdiak/Shutterstock.com; p. 24 Gajus/Shutterstock.com; p. 25 StevenRussellSmithPhotos/Shutterstock.com; p. 27 Comstock Images/Stockbyte/Getty Images; p. 29 (top) Hamiza Bakirci/Shutterstock.com; p. 29 (bottom) Danielle Donders/Moment/Getty Images.

Printed in the United States of America

CPSIA compliance information: Batch #CW16GS: For further information contact Gareth Stevens, New York, New York at 1-800-542-2595.

CONTENTS

Words in the glossary appear in **bold** type the first time they are used in the text.

MY NEW CLUB

My Bird-Watching Checklist

- ☑ a place to see chickadees
- ☑ binoculars
- ☑ a journal and pencil
- ☑ a camera
- ☑ books about chickadees
- ☑ a computer to look up facts and hear calls and songs

Today, I joined a bird-watching club at the community center. I like birds, but I don't know much about them. I thought this would be a great way to learn—and make new friends, too!

The club focuses on one kind of bird for a few weeks. Each week, we meet and share notes about what we observe and find out about the bird. The bird we're watching now is the chickadee. Luckily, I see those all the time in my backyard!

I'll write down what I learn in my journal, so I can remember what I want to share with the club.

A BIRD WITH A CAP

There are several species, or kinds, of chickadees, such as the Carolina chickadee, mountain chickadee, chestnut-backed chickadee, and boreal chickadee. But where I live, the most common chickadee is the black-capped chickadee. This cute little bird looks like it's wearing a black cap and has white "cheeks." It also has grayish feathers on its body. It's small. It weighs about the same as three pennies!

Black-capped chickadees are the most numerous chickadees. I found a map that shows where they live. Here's what it looks like.

Black-capped chickadees live as far north as Alaska and into the northern United States.

BACKYARD CHICKADEE

Important Bird!

Black-capped chickadees are the state bird of Maine and Massachusetts. They're also the official bird of New Brunswick, Canada. People must really like them!

Black-capped chickadees like to live in parks and forests, usually near the edge. They like people's backyards, too, especially if there's a bird feeder there and a place they can build a nest. My backyard has a few trees and several bird feeders near a window where I can see them.

I saw a chickadee in the backyard today. I didn't realize it would be so funny to watch. It likes to hop instead of walk.

A chickadee sometimes hangs upside down from a feeder or tree branch.

9

CHICKADEE MUSIC

What a Chickadee's Call May Mean

- I'm scared!
- Stay away from me!
- A predator is coming!
- The predator is gone. Phew!

I just got back from the bird-watching club. The president brought in a **recording** of a chickadee's call. It sounded like this: "Chick-a-dee-dee-dee!" I guess that's how the bird got its name! It also **whistles** some songs like: "Fee-bee!" or "Fee-bee-ee!" These can sound different depending where the chickadee lives.

Now, I have the window open to hear a chickadee in my backyard. I just heard it! I have to go find my binoculars to try to find it. I'll write more later!

Male chickadees sing more than female chickadees, especially in winter.

11

MAKING A HOME

I spotted the chickadee! It was **peeking** out of a hole in a tree in our backyard. Then it flew away, and I saw a second head peek out. That must be its **mate**.

My friend Dan told the bird-watching club that female chickadees build nests in tree holes like the one in my backyard. It might be an old woodpecker hole that the mates made larger. The female uses moss, grass, and animal fur to make the nest soft. The male helps by bringing her food to eat.

Nesting Box

This is a picture of a nesting box in my neighbor's backyard. A chickadee made its home there! You can buy or make one of these.

Chickadee nests are high off the ground, from 5 to 20 feet (1.5 to 6 m).

CHICKADEE CHOW

A Chickadee's Menu

caterpillars
spiders
snails
bugs
berries
fruit
nuts
seeds

Since I can't see into their home, it'll be easier to watch chickadees if I feed them at the bird feeder. I looked online to find out what kinds of food they like. I was surprised to learn they eat a lot of bugs. Luckily, they eat seeds, too. Those I can buy at the store. They like sunflower seeds as well as peanuts.

Chickadees like to hide food for later. They can remember thousands of hiding places—wow! I'll have to share that fact with my club.

Chickadees also like suet. That's animal fat mixed with seeds, grains, nuts, and fruit.

CHICKADEE EGGS

The male chickadee has been flying back to the nest a lot with food. The female hasn't been around much. I think she laid her eggs. My book says female chickadees often lay between six and eight eggs once a year, between April and August. The eggs are white with reddish brown dots. Each is only about 1/2 inch (1.3 cm) long.

The mother chickadee sits on the eggs to keep them warm until they **hatch**. This is called incubation. It takes about 12 or 13 days for chickadee eggs to hatch.

I can't wait to see the baby chickadees!

17

CHICKADEE CHICKS

Chickadee Chick Timeline

- hatch from eggs after 12 or 13 days of incubation

- eyes begin to open about 7 days old

- grow feathers by 12 days old

- learn to fly between 14 and 18 days old

The eggs have hatched. I know because both the mother and father chickadees have been leaving and coming back with food. The chicks have to eat a lot because they grow so fast. They eat a few times every hour—usually bugs and caterpillars.

When chickadee chicks are born, they have some **down** on their body, but not much. The mother has to stay near to keep them warm. When the chicks have enough warm feathers, the mother starts leaving the nest with the father to find food.

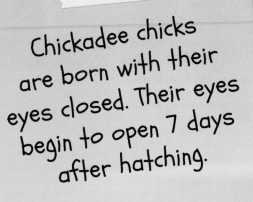

Chickadee chicks are born with their eyes closed. Their eyes begin to open 7 days after hatching.

FLEDGLINGS

Chickadee Fledgling
Call to Parents

sounds like

"Chee-bee!
Chee-bee!"

or

"Feed me!
Feed me!"

This morning, I saw six chickadee chicks learning to fly. I learned this is called "fledging" at my club meeting. The chicks must be about 16 days old, since this is when they normally fledge. They looked like good flyers—but not good landers!

I was surprised to see that the family didn't go back to the nest. However, they all stayed together. The little ones are still being fed, but they peck at the ground, too. They're practicing finding their own food.

Chickadee fledglings, chickadees that have just grown their flying feathers, look like adults, but just a bit smaller.

CHICKADEE ENEMIES

The chicks are gone. One day the family was together, and the next day it was just the mother and father. I was worried that a predator got to the little ones. Owls, hawks, and **shrikes** eat chickadees.

I asked the club president what she thought had happened. She told me that young chickadees usually find their own territory by the time they're 5 or 6 weeks old. They'll stay there the rest of their lives, find mates, and have their own families.

Chickadees may hiss if they see enemies like this hawk approach their nest.

STICKING AROUND

Black-capped chickadees don't usually **migrate**, even though they may live in cold places. They form flocks of up to 10 in winter. The flock works together to find a good food supply in the snow and cold. When a chickadee in a flock finds something tasty, it calls out to the others.

Some other bird species follow chickadees around because they're so good at finding food! When winter arrives, I'll have to remember to fill the bird feeder a lot, so we can feed the hungry birds.

Chickadees can lower their body temperature in winter, so they don't have to work as hard at keeping warm. That's a good trick!

25

CHICKADEES CHIP IN

spread seeds

eat pesky bugs

How They Help

make homes for other animals

I thought I was helping chickadees by feeding them. It turns out they're helping me, too!

Today, an ornithologist (or-nuh-THAH-luh-juhst)—someone who studies birds—came to speak to our club. She said that chickadees help the **environment** in a lot of ways. They spread seeds throughout their habitat, helping grow new plants. They eat bugs that can harm plants. Also, when they make their homes in trees, they prepare the space for other animals to use later.

The ornithologist showed us how to **identify** several kinds of birds today.

MY FAVORITE BIRD

Chickadee Hand Feeding:

1) Place a glove on the feeder with birdseed in it.
2) Begin standing still near the feeder each day, so the birds get used to you being there.
3) Remove the seed from the feeder.
4) Put on the glove with seeds in it. Stand still near the feeder.
5) Watch a chickadee hop into your hand!

Today at the bird-watching club, I learned how to get a chickadee to eat from my hand. I'm going to wait until it's cold outside, because the birds will be hungrier and bolder. I can't wait to try!

I've learned so much about chickadees the past few weeks. I think the black-capped chickadee has become my favorite bird. Bird-watching is a fun hobby that anyone can do. You never know what you'll see or learn next!

Many birds are afraid of people, but chickadees don't have as much fear—as you can see!

29

GLOSSARY

binoculars: handheld lenses that make objects seem closer

down: the soft, fluffy first feathers of a young bird

environment: the natural world in which a plant or animal lives

hatch: to break out of an egg

identify: to find out the name or features of something

journal: a book in which one writes down what happens to them or their thoughts

mate: one of two animals that come together to make babies

migrate: to move from one area to another for feeding or having babies

peek: to take a quick look at something, especially in a secretive way

recording: a copy of sounds that can be played again and again

shrike: a brown or gray songbird with a hooked beak

whistle: to make a sound by blowing breath through the mouth

FOR MORE INFORMATION

Books

Alderfer, Jonathan. *National Geographic Kids Bird Guide of North America: The Best Birding Book for Kids from National Geographic's Bird Experts.* Washington, DC: National Geographic, 2013.

Earley, Chris G. *Birds A to Z.* Buffalo, NY: Firefly Books, 2009.

Zelaya, Carol. *Emily Waits for Her Family.* Oregon City, OR: Richlee Publishing, 2008.

Websites

Black-Capped Chickadee
www.audubon.org/field-guide/bird/black-capped-chickadee
See beautiful photos of chickadees.

Black-Capped Chickadee
www.biokids.umich.edu/critters/Parus_atricapillus/
Many questions about chickadees are answered here.

INDEX